MOTORISTS WISE
SIMONIZ
Makes Cars Stay Beautiful

ADVERTISING BARNS

Vanishing American Landmarks

WILLIAM G. SIMMONDS

MBI

DEDICATION

To my best friend,
Carla Simmonds

This edition first published in 2004 by Motorbooks International, an imprint of MBI Publishing Company, Galtier Plaza, Suite 200, 380 Jackson Street, St. Paul, MN 55101-3885 USA.

Motorbooks International titles are also available at discounts in bulk quantity for industrial or sales-promotional use. For details write to Special Sales Manager at Motorbooks International Wholesalers & Distributors, Galtier Plaza, Suite 200, 380 Jackson Street, St. Paul, MN 55101-3885 USA.

ISBN 0-7603-2083-7

Endpaper: An old Simoniz barn. *Library of Congress*

On the front cover: Mail Pouch barns still dot the countryside throughout the Midwest. This one is on Route 62 in Holmes County, Ohio.

On the frontispiece: This barn, advertising Old Loyalty tobacco, is one of a few that pitched this product. Its home is along Route 421 in Ripley, Indiana.

On the title page: Most advertising barns displayed Mail Pouch Tobacco's "Treat Yourself to the Best" slogan, but plenty also urged travelers to "See 7 States from Rock City," like this barn on Route 64 in Wayne County, Tennessee. Rock City Gardens is a mountaintop attraction in Chattanooga, Tennessee.

On the back cover: As the years have passed, and the United States has become more of an urbanized country, barns like this one in Coffee County, Tennessee, remind us of the time when life was spent on the farm.

Edited by Leah Noel
Designed by William G. Simmonds

Printed in Hong Kong

Contents

INTRODUCTION
A Road Less Traveled

I'm not sure why I've always loved barns. I don't live on a farm. I don't have any farming connections. I haven't experienced much of the agricultural world firsthand. Nevertheless, I, like many other city folk, find the site of an old family homestead—complete with a weathered farmhouse, silo, and barn—comforting. Comforting because these scenes provide a glimpse into a hard-working, self-sufficient, and seemingly honest way of life. And comforting because that's a lifestyle we all can admire. That's why I started taking a closer look at these treasures of rural America every time I took a drive through the country.

Along the way, I became interested in barns that advertised Mail Pouch Tobacco. Many of them dot my home state of Ohio, so I started trying to find and photograph them as I traveled around. One day, I grabbed my camera and headed for one that was close to my northeast Ohio home. As I approached, with the evening light just right for snapping a few photos, I was eager to capture this great piece of history on film. But when I got to where the barn was supposed to be, the structure was gone. Only its foundation and a few broken boards were left. Disappointed, I drove home.

I thought about the other Mail Pouch barns that I had found in my journeys and wondered how many more might be gone now too. A few weeks went by, and I couldn't get the thought of that torn-down barn out of my head. It slowly gnawed away at me. How could anyone tear down such a neat, old barn—a timeless icon of rural Americana?

Opposite: The best place to look for advertising barns is alongside idyllic country roads, such as Route 14 in Wirt County, West Virginia, where this Mail Pouch barn makes its home. *Above:* Some of the businesses advertised on these barns no longer exist, but this barn on Route 231 in Martin County, Indiana, still promotes Line's Clothing.

Above: Some advertising barns offer helpful directions to the wayward traveler, such as this one in Rockcastle County, Kentucky. *Below:* This barn's Dr. Pepper sign is now obscured by a more modern metal sign advertising Diet-Rite Cola.

I soon decided that it was high time to see if other local advertising barns I knew of were still standing.

Thankfully, many still were. A few were showing their age, though. Their roofs were sagging, and their signs were fading away like a distant memory. How many more could I find before they too were either torn down to make room for another subdivision or lost to the ravages of time? Would anyone else notice when they just disappeared? I loaded my camera bag with film, threw my state maps in the car, and began my project to preserve them on film.

At first, I thought I'd do a few day trips, just in the immediate area to see what else I could find. I marked my map with a highlighter to make sure I didn't retrace my travels and documented where I found the best barns. Soon, after spending many hours in my car and studying my tattered map, my day trips turned into weekend adventures, then they became extended weekend jaunts, and eventually turned into vacation days spent searching for these forgotten relics. Whenever I went to visit my sister and her husband, who live in Cincinnati, I took a different route. What was normally a five-hour trip on the freeway turned into an all-day excursion on the back roads. Sometimes I found new barns; sometimes I didn't. Most of the time, one discovery led to another. The hunt went on and on. I was loving it.

I decided to expand my search. I contacted the Mail Pouch Tobacco Company in Wheeling, West Virginia, to see if it could help me out with locating more barn sites. Well, Mail Pouch gave me a partial list of barns that used to carry the company logo, and these barns were spread around several states. Then those who cared for the company's archives shared news clippings and information that would keep me busy researching Mail Pouch barns for years. I thought with all of this stuff starting to pile up that I should make a book out of it.

As my travel spread, I came across many other kinds of advertising barns. Some were kin to Mail Pouch, various

Unfortunately the makeshift supports on this West Virginia barn weren't enough to keep it standing. It has now collapsed.

The Bloch Brothers Tobacco Company used barns to promote many of its products, not just Mail Pouch Tobacco. This barn on Route 78 in Noble County, Ohio, hosts a rare ad for WOW tobacco.

products of the Bloch Brothers Tobacco Company that touted the company's Kentucky Club and WOW tobacco and its Melo Crown cigar brand. I had to shoot those barns too. Then, I'd happen upon barns, sheds, and outbuildings pitching clothing, furniture, automotive services, and other products. Eventually, I headed south to Kentucky, Tennessee, the Carolinas, Georgia, and Alabama to seek out the famous Rock City barns. These beauties—emblazoned with the slogan "See 7 States from Rock City, Atop Lookout Mt., Chattanooga, Tenn."—immediately became my favorites. Then I found barns that heralded other local tourist sites: Sequoyah Caverns in Alabama, Ruby Falls in Chattanooga, and Meramec Caverns in Stanton, Missouri.

Each of these barns had a story to tell. Each, with its unique style, condition, color, age, and location, had its own personality. Was it a well-kept building still serving a valued function and a source of pride on the family farm? Or was it deserted, in a state of disrepair, and slowly collapsing into the soil? I especially enjoy photographing the weathered barns—the ones with weeds growing up around the foundation and boards missing, surrounded by old tractors and forgotten farm equipment rusting away in the shadows. These barns have an unspoken past. They made me appreciate the days when traveling on small two-lane highways—through winding curves, pastoral landscapes, and quaint small towns—was the way we all saw the country.

Over the eight years, 15 states, and 45,000 miles I covered, I spent a lot of time reflecting on what I saw. Beautiful, scenic countryside, paired with lovely, prosperous small towns that had renovated their distinctive buildings to showcase the pride of their Main Street. But I also saw many blighted and economically depressed areas. Many cities and towns were barely surviving, and the farms surrounding

The greatest number of Mail Pouch barns are in Ohio. This one is on Route 30 in Wayne County.

After Mail Pouch barns started popping up all over the country, other businesses decided that barns made great advertising billboards. This one in northern Alabama, which heralds both Rock City Gardens and Sequoyah Caverns, was tendered by the legendary sign painter Clark Byers.

them had been abandoned. I wondered about the people who had once made their living off the land and who had agreed to let their barns advertise a particular product.

Sometimes, I got to meet those barn owners. I was a total stranger, but many of them greeted me with a welcome smile and a warm hello. Some folks even invited me into their homes or offered me a spot on the front porch to talk about the history of the farm or just chat about the weather or current events. On one occasion, a farmer shared his family photo album with me as if I were a long-lost relative.

This book celebrates these people and their barns but also serves as a record of all those barns I have photographed that are gone now. They have vanished, and others showcased in these pages will probably join them in time. So enjoy them, in their understated beauty and humbleness, both within these pages and out on the road.

Left: Both this Pennsylvania barn and its sign are tattered from years of exposure to the elements. *Below:* This Meramec Caverns barn in Indiana also shows years of wear and tear.

Above: Hillside Tobacco was advertised only on a few barns, including this one on Route 67 in Knox County, Indiana. *At right:* A weathered Mail Pouch barn on Route 160 in Somerset County, Pennsylvania.

This rustic Kentucky Pipe Tobacco barn is one of the many that have collapsed after becoming a victim of Mother Nature.

CHAPTER ONE

'Treat Yourself to the Best'

The face of American transportation changed forever at the turn of the century. With the invention of an economical gas-powered vehicle built for the masses, everyone could travel the countryside farther and faster than ever before. Yet in the days before the superhighways, traffic moved at a slower pace, along two-lane state routes that linked city to city and town to town.

It was on these thoroughfares that Aaron and Samuel Bloch, founders of the Mail Pouch Tobacco Company in Wheeling, West Virginia, decided to concentrate their barn advertising campaign. Their simple idea of using large painted letters on the side of a barn to sell a product now seems quaint and out of place in our twenty-first century technology-driven world. But for the Blochs, it was a stroke of genius. They started the barn-painting campaign in the late 1890s, before Henry Ford's Model T made its debut. The campaign became an economical way to market their revolutionary new product—chewing tobacco—to the South's rural-based society. With the right placement, farmers, miners, steelworkers, and blue-collar laborers who worked throughout the Ohio Valley would see the large signs and be reminded to give Mail Pouch a try.

The strategy worked, helping to make their "West Virginia Coleslaw," as it was nicknamed, very popular. Thus began America's most successful and oldest continuous outdoor advertising campaign, the Mail Pouch Tobacco barn. These barns weren't the Bloch brothers' only promotional

Above: This Ohio farm's old tractor gave out years ago, but its Mail Pouch barn still stands. *Opposite:* This Mail Pouch barn has been beautifully restored and stands just east of Lanesville, Indiana, on Route 62.

Above: Some Mail Pouch barns got twice the coverage, being painted on more than one side. *Opposite:* A peaceful scene in Ohio's Muskingum County.

"Treat Yourself to the Best," a phrase one Mail Pouch sign painter came up with, became the most common slogan painted on Mail Pouch barns. *Zimmerman collection*

method, though. They used newspapers, trade cards, point-of-purchase displays, and trolley signs to promote their product. They even capitalized on the fact that the daily mail delivery was a welcome sight to local townspeople by using the post office mailbag as their packaging and product logo. In 1896, Aaron Bloch added another hook to entice customers: He decided to place coupons for free merchandise—including everything from jewelry and watches to household goods and furniture—into the Mail Pouch packs.

But it's the Mail Pouch barn, the best known of advertising barns, that has lasted more than 100 years. While many Mail Pouch barns have been demolished as a result of encroaching urbanization or have fallen into disrepair, others still have the vivid colors that urge travelers to "Chew Mail Pouch Tobacco. Treat Yourself to the Best." Through the years, these rustic billboards have become treasured by those who see them as a vital piece of Americana, something as nostalgic and important as a Norman Rockwell painting.

The surviving Mail Pouch barns are mostly found along the rural routes of the Midwest. Ohio has more Mail Pouch barns than any other state, with the numbers in West Virginia, Pennsylvania, and Indiana trailing close behind. At the height of the Mail Pouch program, a total of four two-man crews worked year-round to paint barns from New Jersey to Florida, north into Minnesota, and west to California, Oregon, Washington, Colorado, and New Mexico. Through the 100-year history of the program, the sign has been painted an estimated 50,000 times.

Barns were selected as Mail Pouch candidates if they had an expansive, windowless side and could be seen easily from well-traveled routes. The best barns were the ones sitting on the curve of a road, where the sign would hit the oncoming motorist right between the eyes as the driver came around the bend. Depending on the structure and its visibility, the logo could be painted on one side, both sides, or the front, but a barn with the Mail Pouch sign painted on three or four sides is a rare sight. Once painted, these barns often

On this barn on Route 322 in Ashtabula County, Ohio, the Mail Pouch sign has blended with a May Company sign.

became directional beacons. "If you follow that road, and turn left at the Mail Pouch barn, it will take you to town," a farmer would say to a lost motorist.

Advance men or the paint crews working the area negotiated the lease deals with farmers to paint the barns. They usually paid farmers anywhere from $1 to $10 a year to allow their barns to be Mail Pouch billboards, and sometimes the farmers received free products and magazine subscriptions as payment. They also got at least one side of their barns, where the sign was, painted for free. And Mail Pouch got a great advertisement without spending much on materials—a smart business plan that helped keep promotional costs down. But in the beginning, it was difficult to convince farmers to let their barns be painted with this tobacco sign. Over time, having a Mail Pouch sign became something of a status symbol. Eventually, hundreds volunteered their barns for the ad space, or in a total switch even offered to pay the company to put the sign on their property.

When passing through West Virginia, home of the Mail Pouch Tobacco Company, every bend in the road can bring another Mail Pouch barn into view.

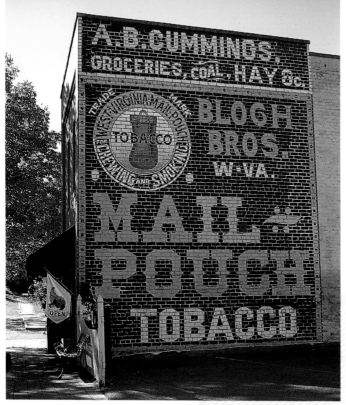

Above: In addition to using barns, Aaron and Samuel Bloch also pitched their product on buildings in town. In 1902, this sign was painted in Jonesboro, Tennessee. The sign was rediscovered in the 1960s when an adjacent building was torn down. *Below:* A Mail Pouch barn in Hampshire County in West Virginia sports the unusual "Regular or Sweet" slogan.

Once a barn was painted with an advertising sign, it became fair game for other contractors and painters to try to paint over it with a new product advertisement. If the sign contract had expired and the owner agreed, a fresh new Mail Pouch sign would cover the previous one. Left unattended, the new sign eventually weathered and started to blend in with the original advertisement. Today, some of these barns with multilayered signs are difficult to interpret, as the various letters have melded together and become unreadable.

Over the years, the design featured on the Mail Pouch barn saw slight changes. The early Mail Pouch signs included a yellow border with black dots spaced 12 inches apart within the stripe. The dots were used to calculate how many square feet the sign painters had covered so they could be paid accordingly. The sign would often include a picture of the mailbag logo and the phrase, "For Chewing and Smoking." The most common Mail Pouch design was created circa 1910. It used large yellow block-style letters for "Mail" and "Pouch" on one line, with smaller yellow letters spelling out "Tobacco" underneath. Even smaller-sized white letters spelled out "Chew" and "Treat Yourself to the Best" upon a black background that had a light blue border. A rarer design was the red-painted Mail Pouch barn. On it, the yellow Mail Pouch letters were accented with a black drop shadow and framed with a white border. This letter-painting style was more laborious to complete, and the bright red color did not wear as well as the black. That's why only a very small percentage of Mail Pouch barns were painted in this fashion. Occasionally, barns featured the word *Chew* painted in script or *Tobacco* brushed in lowercase lettering. Even more unusual barns showcased different Mail Pouch slogans, such as "Regular and Sweet" or "Chewing Serves to Steady the Nerves."

The company product line expanded in 1938 with the creation of a sweet-type chewing tobacco called WOW. In 1939, the Bloch brothers purchased the historic August

Pollack Company of Wheeling, West Virginia, adding cigars once again to their product line. Both WOW tobacco and Melo Crown stogie barns began to appear shortly after this. In 1943, Bloch Brothers purchased the Kentucky Club Pipe Tobacco line from another company. All these additional tobacco products became part of the barn advertising campaign, although to a lesser degree. Kentucky Club barns were covered with this message: "Smoke Kentucky Club. It Never Tires the Taste." The WOW barn sign consisted of a large white circle behind the center of the letter O, creating a bull's-eye look. This product was short-lived, only existing about 10 years. So fewer barns advertised WOW, and today these barns are considered a rare find. As a rule, most of these product lines often shared barn advertising space with the Mail Pouch message.

Maurice Zimmerman—an early Mail Pouch 'paint signer'—on the scaffold of a WOW tobacco barn. *Zimmerman collection*

The Kentucky Club Pipe Tobacco barns were first painted sometime after 1943, when Bloch Brothers Tobacco Company acquired the product. This Kentucky Club barn is on Route 42 in Delaware County, Ohio.

Sometimes trees have have grown up covering this old sign. It becomes more visible in the winter months when leaves don't obscure the message. This barn is on Route 83 in Holmes County, Ohio.

As more barns were painted, regional contractors began hiring and scheduling the crews. They looked for young men who were hardy, ready for a life on the road, and weren't afraid to spend long hours painting on scaffolding that reached high up in the air. Maurice Zimmerman was just such a man. He joined the Mail Pouch painting ranks at the age of 19, in August 1925. He left his Ohio home to join a five-man crew in Syracuse, New York. Over his 30-year career, he ended up painting for other companies too but estimates he rendered the Mail Pouch sign more than 12,000 times.

The men worked nearly year-round from February to December, trying to paint as much as 7,000 to 8,000 square feet of barn siding a week if possible. "At times we averaged 2,000 miles a month," Zimmerman said in his personal memoirs, an oral history compiled by family friend Gerald Carl in 1984. "We called ourselves barn massagers, wall dogs, and barn lizards. We called our overalls skins. After a few days' wear, our skins would get stiff and crusted like suits of armor. When they got so bad we could hardly get them on or bend them at the knees, we would throw them away and buy new ones."

Most often, he noted, painting crews worked as a two-man team, a veteran and a rookie paired together. They were assigned a certain territory for a few weeks and would set up a base camp in a centralized town. There, they would stay in a hotel or boarding house that cost between $2 and $5 a week. Occasionally, the crew would camp in tents or rent a cottage, or even sleep in the truck. At times, a local resident, in an effort to earn a little extra income, would put up the men in a rented room. Some of the boarding houses provided food as part of lodging, and on occasion the farmer who owned the barn being painted would offer a spot at his kitchen table for the crew. And if he were really hospitable, the farmer let the painters eat and stay at his farm. But most of time, the men were on their own, relying on the area restaurants for their meals. After

The barn above promotes both WOW and Mail Pouch Tobacco, while the barn below touts Mail Pouch with a now-antiquated slogan: "Chewing Serves to Steady Nerves."

many years on the road, they knew which places served up the best chow.

"When we were pretty well caught up on our work or on a rainy day, we would drive out on the main highways and lease new locations for signs. We called ourselves 'paint signers' then. We would drive out a few miles, viewing our prospects in one direction, and then return to make our selections from the opposite view. In those days sign locations were fairly easy to find; we always had plenty of work," Zimmerman said. He also noted that most of the time, no one complained about the number of Mail Pouch signs that started dotting the rural landscape. "There weren't many environmentalists in those days to complain about road signs. Oh, once in awhile we'd get some static—usually from women—not about the sign itself, but about chewing tobacco. Didn't want their men folk takin' it up. On a few rare occasions we'd find a lady barn owner who liked to chew."

When coated with fresh paint, a barn's Mail Pouch billboard would remain in good visible condition for three to four years. And after being repainted again and

Maurice Zimmerman (left) with fellow paint crew member Roy Smalley, circa 1928. *Zimmerman collection*

Above: A 1908 photo of Mail Pouch barns right in town in Defiance, Ohio. *Inset:* A circa-1930 photo of a barn located in central Ohio. *Bronson Collection, Center for Archival Collections, Bowling Green State University/Library of Congress*

Above: Occasionally, a barn hunter can find one with a Melo Crown sign. This barn is on Route 550 in Washington County, Ohio. *Inset:* Another Melo Crown sign adorns a barn in Hamilton County, Ohio.

A colorful barn that is home to both Kentucky Club and Mail Pouch advertisements.

again, a barn sign could last for 30 to 40 years. Because barns had to be painted so frequently, often the same painting crews would travel back to their old job sites and meet up with the same farmers and families again. Over time, the painters and farm families became old friends, exchanging news of successful and disappointing harvest seasons, changes in crop planting, and the sorrow of a son that had gone off to war.

For the most part, those long-time relationships took a dramatic turn in October 1965. With the urging of President Lyndon Johnson's wife, Lady Bird, Congress passed the Highway Beautification Act. The legislation attempted to preserve the scenic beauty of the nation's highways by controlling and limiting the construction of billboards within 660 feet of federally funded highways and interstates. The law, designed to clean up the country's cluttered roadways marred by outdoor advertising, forced Mail Pouch to cancel

Above: A friendly visitor hangs out near this barn in Coshocton County, Ohio. *At left:* A retired tractor makes its home next to this barn on Route 88 in Portage County, Ohio.

most of its barn painting plans. As a result, many of the Mail Pouch barns were painted over or destroyed. They were, after all, just advertising signs. Unfortunately for Mail Pouch painting crews, the legislation came during the peak of their work, when more barns featured advertising than ever before. The crews were laid off, except for veteran Mail Pouch sign painter Harley Warrick, the man most often associated with barn painting. He continued to spread paint on a small number of barns on secondary roads that weren't affected by the legislation.

Changes in farming also led to the demise of many of these barns. More and more young people were leaving the farm for good. Upgrades in technology and machinery let

An aging barn among the West Virginia wildflowers on Route 3 in Lincoln County.

large-scale operations take the place of many small family farms, farms that were gobbled up by the competition or by the newest subdivision. Barns left behind in this process were obsolete, the updated farm equipment too large to fit inside them. Many of them fell into disrepair, neglected for years.

In 1969, General Cigar and Tobacco Company purchased Bloch Brothers, and the barn painting program officially ceased. Fortunately, that was short-lived. In 1974, due in part to the efforts of West Virginia Senator Jennings Randolf, the Senate committee on public works amended the Highway Beautification Act. The updated legislation stated that "certain types of outdoor advertising of a unique character," including "signs painted on the sides of rural barns or rocks in natural settings" would be allowed because "some of the advertising has become part of the American folk heritage." The government had accepted Mail Pouch barns as American landmarks. For those who had come to admire these quaint barns, and those who had spent many hours crafting them, this was something they had known all along—these barns were irreplaceable bits of roadside history.

A Ford Model T truck carries the painting crew's supplies as the group works to finish this barn sign. *Zimmerman collection*

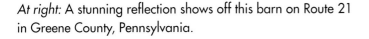

At right: A stunning reflection shows off this barn on Route 21 in Greene County, Pennsylvania.

Both these Mail Pouch barns have survived another winter. The one above is located on Route 460 in Morgan County, Kentucky. The barn at right is in the Wayne National Forest in Washington County, Ohio.

CHEW MAIL POUCH TOBACCO TREAT YOURSELF TO THE BEST

CHEW MAIL POUCH TOBACCO TREAT YOURSELF TO THE BEST

Both large and small rural structures were painted with advertising signs. *Above:* An outbuilding on Route 50 in Athens County, Ohio, painted with a pitch for Mail Pouch. *Inset:* A larger barn with a Hillside Tobacco ad in Spencer County, Indiana.

A Mail Pouch barn on Old Route 50 in Richie County, West Virginia, that has *Chew* painted in the unusual script style.

Left, a Mail Pouch barn stands tall in the plains of Ohio and above a Mail Pouch barn is nestled among the rolling hills of West Virginia.

CHAPTER TWO

Life on the Scaffold

It was an unglamorous job—one that didn't pay very well and wasn't without its dangers. It wasn't only that the job required working high off the ground, on narrow, wobbly scaffolding, with the ever-present chance of falling, that made this a risky career choice. At any minute, a wall dog, as he was called in the early days, could find himself caught up in a severe lightning storm or being pounded by gale-force winds. He worked in all kinds of weather, living with the bone-chilling temperature of a winter's morning and the summer's daylong scorching heat. He could come under attack by a swarm of hornets or bees or even have a chance encounter with an angry bull.

But he faced all of this and still kept plugging away at his task—making a shabby old barn look new again. Harley Warrick, the last and most famous Mail Pouch painter, spent 45 years of his life doing this. He retired in 1992, after rendering the company logo more than 22,000 times on his journeys throughout the American heartland. He was first drawn to the job on a cold February day in 1946, less than a week after returning from serving in the army in Europe.

While he was away, his family had moved to a farm in Guernsey County near Londonderry, Ohio. So Warrick headed there, with the full intention of taking over cow-milking duties. As luck would have it, the farm's dairy barn carried a Mail Pouch advertising sign, which a crew came to paint that week. Warrick watched with great interest as

Above: Two painters take a break while painting a barn in Ashtabula, Ohio, circa 1925. *Opposite:* This weathered Geauga County, Ohio, barn has since collapased, another victim of time and the elements.

Here a painter finishes a huge undertaking, painting a roof and the side of a large Maryland barn. *Library of Congress*

the men worked, and he chatted with them, trading stories. As the crew finished up, the foreman told Warrick he was looking for some more workers. The pay was $28 a week plus square-foot production incentives, which could increase the salary to about $32 a week, not to mention all the Mail Pouch you could chew. But he would have to pay all of his living and food expenses.

Still, Warrick didn't need convincing; he joined the team that day. "It was better than milking 27 head of Jerseys every night and morning. I didn't mind the farm; I just thought this would be better," he said in a 1995 interview. So he filled his duffel bag with clothes, climbed into the panel truck, and headed down the road looking forward to good times and new-found adventures. He thought it would be a temporary job. "I wanted to take about six months off and kick up my

heels a bit," he said. Instead, he kept at it for four decades and became widely known for his trade, eventually being elevated to the status of a revered folk artist.

He trained under another longtime Mail Pouch barn painter, Maurice Zimmerman, who also painted ads for rival Red Man tobacco, Simoniz car wax, Minneapolis Milling Company, and many other companies. Zimmerman painted his last sign in 1975, when he rendered the familiar Mail Pouch letters on a small barn owned by his son Norman. Zimmerman passed away in 1993.

Warrick started his apprenticeship by filling in the backgrounds while the more seasoned painters handled the lettering, but he proved to be a quick learner. Within three months, he became a journeyman painter. "The first few hundred looked like I painted them with my feet," he said. "But after a few thousand or so you begin to get the hang of it."

For the first 20 years, Warrick worked 50 weeks a year, six days a week. He and a partner painted or repainted two to three barns a day, about 700 a year. "If it didn't move, we painted it," he once joked. At one point, Warrick did return home, at age 27, to get married. But his vagabond lifestyle didn't suit his wife, and she told him either to find a new job or a new wife. Warrick said she had a deal. "I told her

The method of painting barns hasn't changed much over the years, as you can see in these photos where both Harley Warrick (below) and another painter tackle the job. *Zimmerman collection, Ray Day*

Dressed in his trademark overalls, Harley Warrick applies the legendary Mail Pouch lettering on a barn located on the southwest Missouri farm of Lowell Davis. *Ray Day*

Above: Maurice Zimmerman also painted for rival Red Man tobacco and Simoniz car wax. *Zimmerman collection*
At right: This barn on Route 281, Somerset County, Pennsylvania, has two Mail Pouch ads.

good jobs were hard to find. My second wife is much more understanding."

The time it took to finish painting a barn depended on the size of the structure and how many men were painting it. For an average-sized barn, a two-man crew could complete the job in about three hours. Then they would sign their names or initials and year completed in the eaves or on the front of the barn as a record of their work. After painting thousands of signs, Warrick honed his skills to where he could paint a large barn by himself in about eight hours.

Zimmerman and Warrick both took the following approach when they started to size up a new paint job: They first stood back and studied the barn's architecture before picking up a paintbrush. "You'd visualize the barn, and picture that sign in your mind," Zimmerman said. After making any minor repair work to the siding, they would put the scaffold in place. Then they would lean 40-foot-tall ladders on the sides of the barn, climb up to the peak, and attach their swing stage or platform from heavy ropes. This 2-foot-wide, 20-foot-long platform gave the painters about a 24-foot-wide spread of barn panel before they needed to lower it to paint the next level.

"Then you'd pick out a board or window or something to use as a guideline," Zimmerman noted. With that in place, he would start at the top, painting C-H-E-W first. Dropping the scaffold down, he and the crew would paint the Mail Pouch slogan next. They would use a horizontal chalk line as a guideline to keep the letters straight. They painted the *P*, the center letter, first. From there, they spaced out the rest of the letters. To paint the word *Tobacco*, the painters also started with the center letter, the *a*, first. Then they would rough in the rest of the letters on each side of it. After creating a rough shape for each of these, the crew would use a diagonal-cut brush filled with the background color to create a sharp, clean edge for the letters. In the process, they never used any sort of stencil to make the letters

uniform. "Stencils are a dirty word to a sign painter," Warrick said in Randy Leffingwell's *The American Barn*. "Besides, every barn is different. [If I used them,] I'd have to have a semitrailer following me full of stencils." Clark Byers, who painted Rock City barns for nearly three decades, agreed, noting, "I sized up roof sections and spaced out the letters. Most of the time I got it right."

For paint, the crews used Dutch Boy white lead, which came in 100-pound kegs. "We opened untold hundreds of those kegs," Zimmerman said, explaining that the paint was then mixed with linseed oil, colored, and stored in 5- and 10-gallon milk cans. For the black paint, a painter would add dry lampblack, a pigment, to the linseed oil to get the right shade. "Then we thinned it with gasoline. That was our paint thinner—gasoline."

"We put it on just as heavy as it would go on. You couldn't make your paint thin because some of those barns would soak it in. It was like painting on a blotter sometimes, and they were very rough," Zimmerman noted. With the right mixture, though, "once that paint got on, there was no getting it off," Byers added. The paint mix could cost as much as $40 a gallon—an expense that Mail Pouch executives balked at—but Warrick once noted that most of the time his crew could get a barn painted in one coat. By only painting one coat, he could keep up his aggressive barn painting schedule, finishing two barns a day, six days a week.

Sometimes, despite Warrick's efforts, the best-laid plans just didn't work out. One time he and a colleague ran out of space as they where finishing a sign. They were forced to continue the letters around the other side of the barn.

"Coming down the road one way, you could read it. But coming the other way, you couldn't," he said when discussing the error. He fixed it by adding a little something extra—the word *Oops!* at the end of the text.

Another oops was misspelling a word. One time while showing off to some observers, Byers tried painting the letters backwards on a See Rock City barn—and it came out See Rock Ctiy instead. "That broke me of backwards painting," he said. Warrick didn't always get things spelled right either, but usually he had purposely made mistakes to be a little mischievous. "I'd put an extra c in tobacco, just to see if anyone was paying attention," he recalled with a smile. After a few letters to Mail Pouch, "about that darn painter that can't spell," he would return and fix the sign, happy to know that the public was still noticing what he was doing.

When the Highway Beautification Act passed in 1965, Warrick continued to paint a limited number of Mail Pouch barns, working with Mail Pouch under only a handshake agreement. He became the sole contractor and was responsible for the leasing and painting of the barns "for reasons of corporate tradition." Most of the time he traveled alone, with a truck full of paint, and spent 8 to 10 hours a day

Warrick stirring the paint for another day on the job.
Ray Day

The longest barn Harley Warrick ever painted was on Route 74 in Ritchie County, West Virginia, while the smallest barns he painted were the ones he made in his workshop.

Right: A John Deere tractor sits in front of this red Mail Pouch barn on Route 197 in Richland County, Ohio. *Below:* A Mail Pouch barn in West Virginia fades into oblivion.

maintaining about 200 Mail Pouch barns in the industrial areas of Ohio, West Virginia, Pennsylvania, and western Maryland. In the process, as the public started to view these barns as nostalgic icons, Warrick became something of a celebrity.

He was featured in hundreds of newspaper articles and magazine stories and traveled to fairs and festivals to demonstrate his skills. His fame increased when he was interviewed on television programs such as *Good Morning, America* and *On the Road with Charles Kuralt*. He even appeared in a Mail Pouch commercial. In 1967, the Smithsonian Institution asked him to be part of its Man and His World exhibit at the Montreal World's Fair. He painted the Mail Pouch sign on a wall during the day and whitewashed it at night so he could repaint it the next day.

The most unusual surface Warrick ever painted was the hide of an elephant. In 1980 a circus came to Wheeling, and Mail Pouch leased space on both sides of the pachyderm. He painted the elephant with watercolors while it lay on its side. "I felt a little foolish," he said, remembering that day. Other unusual places where his work has appeared include tavern or restaurant walls and even some people's family rooms. The largest barn Warrick ever painted is located just north of Pennsboro, West Virginia, and measures 144 feet long. On the other end of the spectrum, the smallest barns he painted were the ones he sold out of his home-side workshop. After he painted his last official Mail Pouch barn in 1991, he didn't stop working entirely. He spent his time building and painting birdhouses and feeders with the Mail Pouch sign.

He also tried to pass on his profession by training new painters over the years, but none chose to stay with the life-on-the-road job. "It's a tough way to make a living," he explained. Even Warrrick's son, Roger, gave it a try, working a summer with his father to help pay for his college education.

The Mail Pouch barn-painting era officially ended when Warrick died on November 25, 2000, at the age of 76. Thankfully, many of the barns he painted live on, as do others that were crafted by Maurice Zimmerman, Clark Byers, Jim Gauer, and many other talented men who traveled the countryside creating colorful legacies. Hopefully, they will continue to stand for years to come as a testament to a man's life work.

This is a rare barn sign that not only sports the Mail Pouch letters, but the famous pack the product came in. Above is a sample tobacco pack circa 1910.

Left: Rays of sunlight cast a golden glow on this barn on Route 33 in Athens County, Ohio. *Above:* A rusted-out pickup becomes part of the landscape around this barn on Route 50 in Garrett County, Maryland.

As the seasons roll from one into another, this red Mail Pouch barn in Ohio weathers the elements and still shows its strong colors. Red Mail Pouch barns aren't seen as often because painting the barn was labor intensive.

At one time, Mail Pouch barns filled the Indiana countryside, but today few are left. This dilapidated one is on Route 6 in Noble County.

The faded Mail Pouch barn above is in Ohio Amish country and the red one in the inset photo is on Route 152 in Wayne County, West Virginia.

Harley Warrick painted this barn in 1998. It's on the Algonquin Mill Historical Site on Route 332 in Carroll County, Ohio.

Warrick stands in front of a freshly painted sign that he worked on as part of a special barn painting informational program held at Malabar Farm State Park in Lucas, Ohio, in September 1997.

This photo shows a very unusual Mail Pouch sign, an oval one, that was painted on a building in Defiance, Ohio, around 1932. *Zimmerman collection*

CHAPTER THREE
A Roadside Attraction

Today you can hop on a super highway and travel virtually coast-to-coast without seeing the real America. Everything you need is conveniently situated at almost any exit. Gas up at a super station, grab a bite to eat at a fast-food restaurant, get a little shut-eye at a nondescript hotel, and slip back on the endless concrete ribbon. If you look for local flavor between exits, you won't find much.

In the days before nonstop freeways, the motoring public traveled on the nation's two-lane state and county roads, which snaked their way through the countryside past local establishments, not brand-name enterprises. These roads had traffic that moved slower than on the 65-plus-mile-per-hour four-lane thoroughfares and made traveling much more of an adventure. They took you right through the center of town, let you see the local sights, and made the diner on the corner the spot where everyone ate, both the hometown folk and those just passing through.

As more and more people got into the car for a vacation or extended trip, these routes became home to tourist-friendly cabins, motels, restaurants, gas stations, amusement parks, and attractions. At the same time, advertising to a large audience was becoming an essential piece of good business. Billboards started popping up along these roads to lure the tourists in, and barns were getting facelifts that made them marketing tools, too.

But vacationers dwindled when the Great Depression hit, and roadside destinations had a hard time staying

Opposite: Old rugged advertising barns often have a lot of character, as this one does on Route 150 in Washington County, Indiana. *Above:* Tourist sites used advertising barns to attract the motoring public. But ones heralding Ruby Falls like this one are seldom seen. This barn is along Interstate 65 in Tennessee.

afloat. Rock City Gardens, located outside of Chattanooga, Tennessee, was among those that struggled to survive. Situated high atop Lookout Mountain, which straddles the state line between Tennessee and Georgia, this geological marvel opened to the public in 1932. Garnet and Frieda Carter developed it. Initially, it was Frieda who saw value in the area known locally as "Rock City." In 1930, following her specifications, workmen laid a series of stepping stone walkways throughout the intricate, narrow passages that wound their way around the boulders and huge rocks on the mountaintop. Along the trails, she planted a wide variety of wildflowers, shrubs, and other plants, carefully placed to resemble nature's own work. She also had rustic bridges constructed to span the area's deep crevices. Statues of gnomes and fairyland characters found homes along the pathways that meandered through 14 scenic acres. They all led to the top of Lookout Mountain, which promised a view of seven different states.

But the mountaintop attraction was not exactly your typical roadside stop. People just didn't happen by. Garnet Carter, a real estate entrepreneur and developer of the first nationally recognized miniature golf course, decided he needed to find a better way to get travelers up to Rock City.

After meeting with Fred Maxwell, owner of a Chattanooga advertising agency, he decided in the mid-1930s that painting barns would be his best promotional tool. So he and Maxwell launched a barn painting campaign similar to the one that Mail Pouch Tobacco had conducted for the previous 35 years.

Luckily enough, Clark Byers, a 22-year-old self-taught sign painter was already working for Maxwell's agency, so he got the task of approaching farmers and asking them if he could paint a sign on the roof or the side of their barns. When Byers asked Carter what message he was to paint on these barns, he was given a piece of paper with three simple words on it: "See Rock City." So that's what he painted on his first barn near Kimball, Tennessee.

At first Carter and Maxwell picked the sites for the new signs. "They drove up and down the roads, making notes on the barns they wanted to use," Byers said in an interview in the 1990s. "Then they told me to get the owner's permission to paint the roofs or sides of the buildings." In return, Byers offered the farmers free passes to the tourist spot or other Rock City promotional items. Sometimes he paid them between $3 and $5 a year to host a Rock City sign on their barns. Later on, Byers himself would pick the locations

Right: Many barns in the South promote Rock City Gardens, a mountaintop tourist site in Chattanooga, Tennessee. This barn sits along Route 441 in Sevier County, Tennessee. *Opposite:* Meramec Caverns, a Missouri site along historic Route 66, was another attraction that was the subject of barn advertising. This barn is on Route 6 in Noble County, Indiana.

High Falls in Rock City Gardens Atop Lookout Mountain

These tourist sites also used other promotional tools to get the word out about them. Among those early items were postcards, like this one above from Rock City Gardens and inset from Ruby Falls.

for new barns. "I couldn't pass up a good roof," he said. "I felt obligated to Garnet Carter to find the best roof I could." Soon, Byers created more catchy phrases and added them to the barns and sheds that dotted the South. A few included "Beautiful Beyond Belief," "The Eighth Wonder of the World," "When You See Rock City, You See the Best." But no matter what slogan he used, Byers kept the design simple. He used large, bold white lettering on a black background, often including directions or a route number that travelers easily could see at a glance from the road. From as far north as Michigan, as west as Texas, and as south as Florida, these rural billboards did the trick. More and more people were making their way to the top of Lookout Mountain and seeing Rock City.

With help, Byers averaged painting up to three barns a day and was paid $40 a barn, which he shared with his helper. He mostly chose barns with wooden pitched roofs, but he also painted shingled barns, which were the hardest

Above: Rooftop painters use their balancing skills to get the job done on a Rock City sign. *Left:* A Ruby Falls barn that also has its roof painted with a Meramec Caverns sign, which is on the other side.

Clark Byers, the longtime Rock City barn painter, poses in front of a recently painted Rock City rooftop.
Rock City Gardens

to cover with paint. Like his tobacco barn-painting counterpart of the time, Harley Warrick, Byers made many friends during his barn-painting days. He spent a lot of time talking with gracious farmers as he painted barn rooftops. He also was a hard worker, often toiling into the evening darkness and occasionally finishing up a paint job with the aid of his truck's headlights.

In 1965, Clark Byers somehow found time in his busy schedule to develop his own family campground and tourist destination, Sequoyah Caverns. Located in northern Alabama, 35 miles south of Chattanooga, Sequoyah Caverns was named after the Cherokee Indian chief Sequoyah, who fought alongside Sam Houston and Andrew Jackson in the War of 1812. The site is home to Looking Glass Lake, an underground pool that reflects thousands of rock formations. After nearly 30 years painting Rock City barns and seeing how effective they were, Byers already knew the perfect way to make his attraction, complete with a "Sam Houston, 1830" inscription on one of its rock formations, more well

known. So he began painting barns promoting the caverns throughout the area.

In the height of his barn-painting days, Byers and his crew painted as many as 900 signs in 19 states. His career came to an end in 1986, after he nearly lost his life while working on a painting job. He was shocked by a downed power line that was draped over a sign he was repainting. He remained hospitalized long enough to reconsider his profession. After hanging up his brushes, he concentrated on running his campground, eventually retiring to a small farm in Georgia. He passed away in February 2004 at the age of 84.

Only about 100 of the Rock City barns Clark painted are left today, but a select number still get a facelift every few years by his replacement, Jerry Cannon. They continue to be enjoyed by a new generation of tourists. In fact, Rock City ushered in a new era in 2000, when one of its barn signs advertised its Web site, www.seerockcity.com. It was the first time barn-side advertising came face to face with the information super highway.

It would be difficult to get lost looking for Rock City when you've got these helpful signs pointing the way. This one is on Route 411 in Monroe County, Tennessee.

A Rock City barn sits in the misty morning rain along Route 79, in Montgomery County, Tennessee.

Another beautiful and unique tourist spot is Ruby Falls, known as "the jewel of Lookout Mountain." Not only is it near Rock City, but it also has its own advertising barns as well. Other than the signs, what attracts tourist to the site is its magnificent waterfall, measuring 145 feet high and located 1,120 feet inside the mountain. It was discovered in the late 1920s when Leo Lambert, a local spelunker, was trying to develop the historic Lookout Mountain Cave—once used as a rendezvous spot by Native Americans and Confederate and Union soldiers—into a tourist destination. Lambert named the falls in honor of his wife, Ruby. He decided to develop two caves for tourists to visit, the original cave and the one with Ruby Falls. Over the next five years, he offered tours of both caves, but Ruby Falls proved to be the more popular so he closed the original cave in 1935.

Unfortunately, most of the barns that advertised Ruby Falls no longer exist, but a few fairly new ones still appear along well-traveled roads and within sight of the interstates near the attraction.

Meramec Caverns was another tourist attraction that opened during the tough economic times of the Depression and used barns as a way to let travelers know its location. Situated along the banks of the Meramec River, one hour west of St. Louis in Stanton, Missouri, the caverns include the largest single cave formation in the world, with more than 26 miles of underground passages on seven different levels. Believed to be one of the first known caves in America, it contains a vast deposit of potassium nitrate, or saltpeter, which is used to produce gunpowder. The French were the first to mine the cave around 1720, and it was mined again during the Civil War. It was used by slaves as a stop on the Underground Railroad, and it was said to be a hideout of outlaw Jesse James.

As a boy, Lester B. Dill, who grew up in Stanton, explored many of the area caves and made small change giving tours. A showman at heart, Dill purchased what was known as Saltpeter Cave in 1935. He renamed it Meramec Caverns, promoting the site as "the Greatest Show under Earth." After the caverns opened, Dill took a trip to Florida. Along the way, he spotted barns with the owners' names painted on the roofs. He liked what he saw and wondered if something like that would work for his attraction. Because Meramec Caverns was a mom-and-pop business, he knew he couldn't afford the big billboards that advertising firms created. So he decided to give the barn sign a try.

He painted the first few himself with the simple black-and-white message "Meramec Caverns, Stanton, Mo." Years later additional colors and the highway numbers were added. He paid the farmers who owned the barns with passes to the cave. The signs brought people in, so he concluded that with more signs he'd get even more tourists to Meramec Caverns. Capitalizing on the fact that Route 66 was a destination in itself, the first few barns with the caverns signs were located along the Mother Road. Eventually nine signs were painted along Route 66. With these barns, Meramec Caverns became a significant part of the nostalgia that still surrounds the 2,400-mile highway today.

Meramec Caverns, advertised at right and below, are believed to be the one-time hangout of outlaw Jesse James.

Once there were about 350 Meramec barns spread throughout the South and Midwest. Several men painted the signs after Dill did the first few, but when Jim Gauer was hired in 1956, he became the only barn painter spreading the message about the caverns. After serving during World War II, Gauer found himself in San Francisco, where he spent five years with a crew that painted the Golden Gate Bridge. Family brought him back to his hometown of Stanton, Missouri. "I was looking for a job," he said in a 1994 interview in the *Route 66 Association of Illinois* magazine. "My brother told me I might be able to get one down at Meramec. When I got here, they hired me right away. And I've been here ever since." Gauer started out using the traditional rollers and paint brushes but later switched to

Clark Byers shows off his one-of-a-kind Rock City birdhouse-style mailbox. But the U.S. Postal Service rejected it due to its regulations, so Byers ended up just selling them as birdhouses. At left, an old pack of matches promotes the product that can still be purchased today. *Rock City Gardens*

10 Miles to Sequoyah CAVERNS

After spending years painting barns for Rock City Gardens, Clark Byers decided to develop and promote Sequoyah Caverns as his own tourist site. This barn is on Route 11 in Dekalb County, Alabama. *Inset:* Jim Gauer painted the barn signs for Meramec Caverns.

STANTON MO.
MERAMEC
CAVERNS

This Alabama Rock City barn sits inside an auto junkyard on Route 11 in Dekalb County.

spraying on the paint. He traveled with a compressor and 300 feet of hoses. "You have to be careful with the sprayers; they pack 2,000 pounds of pressure," he said. During his career, Gauer traveled about 50,000 miles a year maintaining about 90 barns.

Painting mostly by himself, he usually used five to ten gallons of paint to cover a sign. He finished two to three barns a day. In 38 years, he rendered the sign an estimated 5,000 times. Like the other painters of the time, Gauer enjoyed his visits with the farmers who owned the barns and knew many of the families for decades. He has now been employed at Meramec Caverns for almost 50 years and still does occasional odd jobs.

Neither he nor any other painter has crafted a new Meramec barn sign since 1965. And sadly, only about 88 of the original cavern signs are still standing. They are mostly located along old state byways in Illinois and Missouri. Meramec Caverns has switched its advertising campaign to the modern billboard. Gauer summed it up this way when talking about the old barns: "There aren't too many of them left. It won't be long before we don't have any. I'm sure of that."

For many years advertising barns helped make these tourist attractions successful and now have entered their place in tourism history. In the case of Rock City, the barns are almost as big of an attraction as the gardens themselves. As such, these barn signs continue to be regarded as time-worn images of a past era, revered in the hearts and minds of many Americans.

The "See Rock City" message is spread throughout Tennessee, including on this barn in Monroe County.

Many Rock City barns still display signs that are in good condition, like this one above, which is on Route 41 in Gibson County, Indiana. But the Meramec Caverns barn at left on Old U.S. Highway 68 in Kentucky could use a fresh coat of paint.

This barn on Route 50 in Garrett County, Maryland, sports two advertising signs, one for Smoke Hole Caverns—which is a Seneca Rocks, West Virginia, tourist spot—as well as one for the familiar Mail Pouch Tobacco.

The only part of this Kentucky barn that's not covered in ivy is its rooftop with a Rock City advertisement blazoned across it.

This barn offers travelers plenty to read, with large Rock City and Mail Pouch messages covering its exterior. Unfortunately those passing through Jay County, Indiana, will no longer see this barn, which has since fallen to the ravages of time.
Tom Plimpton

A pink sky cascades around this large Rock City barn on Route 127 in Bledsoe County, Tennessee.

This small Rock City Barn is almost completely hidden from those traveling on Route 150 in Orange County, Indiana.

This old truck almost looks like one that a sign-painting crew could have left behind at this barn on U.S. Highway 11 in McMinn County in Tennessee.

This bold Rock City barn is part of the grounds of the Maker's Mark Distillery in Marion County, Kentucky.

A weathering Rock City barn on U.S. Highway 231 in Owen County, Indiana.

Many barns are no longer seen by the motoring public, as the roadways they are located on are not highly traveled interstates or highways. This barn on Old U.S. Highway 68 is among those seldom-seen sites in Nicolas County, Kentucky.

Snow is obscuring this rooftop ad for Meramec Caverns. The barn—on Route 231 in Martin County, Indiana—also is home to Mail Pouch and Kentucky Club tobacco ads.

Right: This rugged barn does double duty promoting Kent's Truck Stop and Ruby Falls on Route 31 in Robertson County, Tennessee. *Below:* A faded Meramec Caverns rooftop ad in western Ohio.

The main road now bypasses this old barn in Brown County, Ohio.

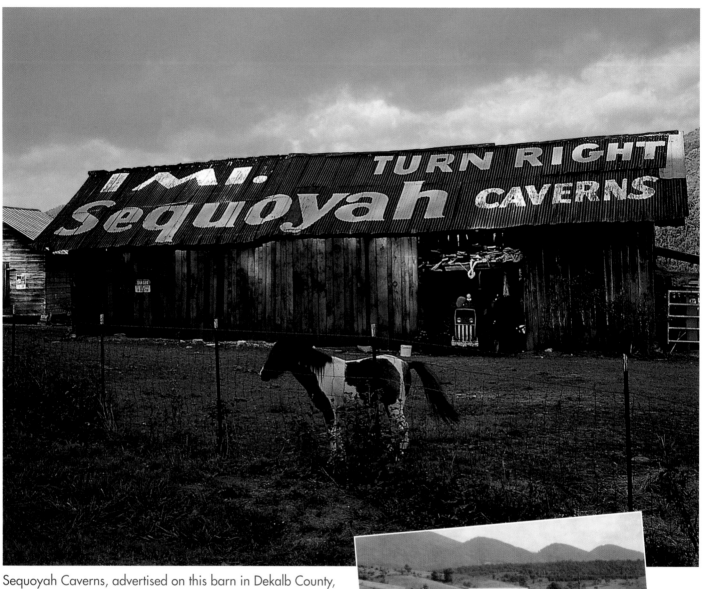

Sequoyah Caverns, advertised on this barn in Dekalb County, is now owned by the Cherokee tribe of northeast Alabama.

This early scene shows a barn pitching Endless Caverns—a New Market, Virginia, attraction—on U.S. Highway 50 in West Virginia. *Author's collection*

A sign wishing Rock City visitors farewell near Interstate 24 in Marion County, Tennessee.

CHAPTER FOUR
Suits and Miracle Cures

While Mail Pouch and Rock City made their barn campaigns wide-reaching and well known, other businesses took a smaller, more local approach when they decided to promote their goods and services via highly visible barns. The advertisements they created mostly were meant to entice the locals or maybe pique the interest of someone just passing through, and pitched anything from beverages and tires to medicine and potato chips.

These barn ads didn't sport uniform designs, nor were they painted by a traveling crew. Most of the time they came into being after a local shop owner decided he needed to boost business and bring the farm folk into town more often. So he'd hire a local painter to create these billboard-like ads on barns throughout the area. Because his business was not only competing with large downtown department stores but also with mail-order catalogs from Sears and Montgomery Wards, he desperately needed the support of area buyers. Unlike a newspaper ad that would be thrown out with the trash, advertising barns provided a promotion 365 days a year at no additional cost.

Some of the items touted on the barns included automotive supplies, soap, bread, beer, colas, groceries, gasoline, banks, and hotels. Other barns offered cures to your ailments. But no matter what product or service was for sale, the message had to be simple and to the point. After

The C. H. Bennett sign above in Monroe, Connecticut, was restored by the barn's owner, while the barn on the opposite page looks a little more dated, especially with a sign advertising Richman's Clothes, a store that sold suits for $22.50.

only a few seconds, passing drivers would need to get their eyes back on the road.

Some of the messages read: "Go to C. H. Bennett for boots, shoes, and rubbers, 367 Main Street" or "Shop at Sieberts, Clothes for the Entire Family." No need for long explanations, the locals knew where to go. One barn in Ohio Amish country displayed a laundry list of goods, including "Quality Meats, Groceries, Quilting Supplies, Amish Hats, Farming Clothes, Shoes, Rural Restaurant, Just Minutes Ahead," plus the name of the store. A few business establishments were bold, deciding that their price was low enough to plaster up for all to see. "Suits Made to Order, Made to Fit, just $24.00," said one. Another-boasted, "Overcoats, $28.00." Now, these signs serve as a permanent record of sorts, something to remind everyone how much inflation has changed things.

Barn signs promoting clothing and shoe stores proved to be the most popular small regional campaigns. They would boast about how many locations the establishments had—"27 Stores to Serve You"—or give directions on how to find them. Sometimes the competition—the large department store downtown—got into the act by using a barn to get its message out. The May Company, at the time one of Cleveland, Ohio's largest and proudest department stores, had barns painted in several rural counties of northeast Ohio. The signs proclaimed May Company as "Ohio's Largest Store" and said "Watch Us Grow." Eventually, the chain of stores sold, and its name changed. Now only a few

This is one rare instance where the store this Ohio barn promoted is still in business, but the barn is long gone.

The May Company entered the Cleveland market in 1899 and used barns as one way to promote its stores. The barn at left is on Route 87 in Trumbull County, Ohio, and the barn below is located in Ashtabula County.

Barns weren't the only rural structures to get the billboard treatment. Occasionally silos were painted to pitch a product. This one, advertising New Era Potato Chips in Portland, Michigan, was restored by the farm owner's son in the mid-1990s.

remaining May Company barn signs remind passing motorists of the store's former existence. Another Cleveland-based clothing store, not to be outdone by Mays, also used ads on select barns. The Richman Brothers Company opened retail outlets selling factory-made men's clothing directly to the customer—the first clothier to do so. The company's simple, large white-lettered signs appeared in Ohio, Pennsylvania, and western New York.

Aside from furniture and clothing, medicine also was a popular product marketed on the sides of barns. Most of the time these advertisements—which popped up in the nineteenth century—heralded products that claimed to cure a host of physical ills. These ads worked because most rural residents had limited access to doctors. Customers often found it easier and cheaper to head to the general store and purchase a bottle or two of a miracle remedy than to make a visit to the doctor. In reality, customers probably felt better only because these medicines were loaded with alcohol, morphine, cocaine, or opium. But other, more legitimate, pharmaceutical products were also promoted on barns. Fletcher's Castoria, a gentle laxative for children, and Black Draught laxative, a product of the Chattanooga Medicine Company, were two that found

rural barn billboards to be valuable marketing tools. An interesting footnote: The Black Draught representative did double-duty as the company salesman and the sign painter.

Dr. R. V. Pierce of Buffalo, New York, also used barns to solicit sales of his medicines, which were mostly geared toward women. Some of those included Dr. Pierce's Favorite Prescription, Pleasant Pellets, and the Golden Medical Discovery, all best-selling mail-order products. His publications, such as the *The People's Common Sense Medical Advisor*, were well read during that time. Initially most of the barns with Dr. Pierce advertisements on them were located near Buffalo, but he did commission a number of them in the Midwest and the West. In fact, historical societies have restored a few located in Oregon, Utah, and Washington.

Of course not all signs were regional in nature. Giant corporations of the day also utilized the barn billboard. Outdoor advertising firms located in the metropolitan areas would represent their major clients such as Firestone or Coca-Cola with signs placed along the familiar country roads. The agencies' location men traveled the countryside in search of good barn locations, often competing with the Mail Pouch painters for a desirable site. After locking up the agreement, paint crews were given sign painting instructions and then sent out with maps to the barns.

Today, most of the barn signs promoting goods or services have faded almost to the point of disappearing. Many of the stores and businesses no longer exist, their advertising campaigns long over. A sharp traveler may be lucky enough catch a glimpse of one of these barn signs tucked away in the shadows of overgrown trees, but the message it gives will be a well-hidden treasure.

Dr. R. V. Pierce promoted many of his medicinal remedies using barns around the Buffalo, New York, area. *Author's collection*

This barn looks like every business in town put its advertisement on it. *Author's collection*

The barn above advertises a Chevrolet dealership in Indiana, while the ad on the rooftop of the barn inset lets travelers know that Harper's Old Country Store is only 700 feet farther down the road on Route 33 in Pendelton County, West Virginia.

Hidden behind these trees, and fading to the point of no return, is a promotion for Smith's Poultry on this barn in LaRue County, Kentucky.

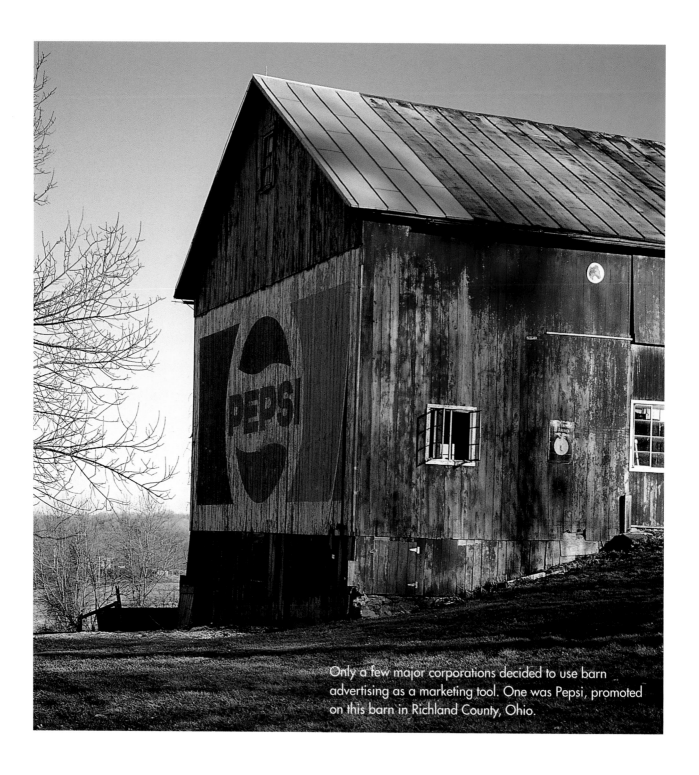

Only a few major corporations decided to use barn advertising as a marketing tool. One was Pepsi, promoted on this barn in Richland County, Ohio.

Not too many Jefferson Island Salt barns exist anymore. They were painted in the late 1950s by Ralph Atkins, the only person to paint the Jefferson Island message. *Background image: Library of Congress*

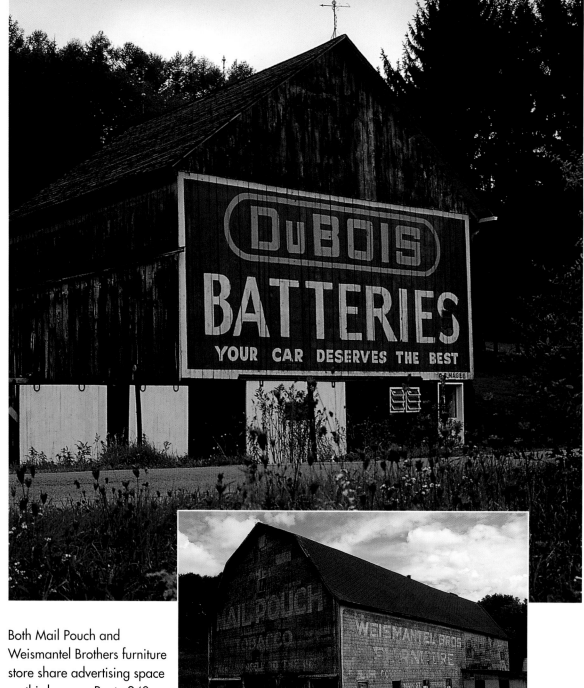

This Dubois Batteries sign is about 50 years old and is near Route 219 in Jefferson County, Pennsylvania.

Both Mail Pouch and Weismantel Brothers furniture store share advertising space on this barn on Route 240 near Springville, New York.

This fading sign told passing motorists that Frisch's Big Boy restaurant was only six miles further down Old U.S. Highway 52 in Hamilton County, Ohio.

This red barn with its McCreary Tires sign blends in beautifully with the fall foliage surrounding Route 13 in Schuyler County, New York.

Bacon in glass jars? Well, that's what this barn is trying to sell passing motorists in Ottowa County, Ohio.

Two adjacent barns filled with shoe and clothing advertisements. *Author's collection*

Instead of being painted directly on this rural outbuilding, this Stroehmann Bread advertisement is really a metal sign that is attached to the building's side.

It's hard to tell what this barn is advertising as its Mail Pouch and Goodrich Tire lettering have faded together.

Siebert's Clothing store still does business in downtown Jasper, Indiana, so this barn may not have lost its marketing value.

Vintage photos showing a 1930s-era advertisement for Lerch Suits (above) in Ohio and Lieter Brothers clothing store in Maryland. *Library of Congress*

The beautiful script lettering used on the Fletcher's Castoria barn at right made this structure a piece of public art. *Author's collection*
Below: The Schoenfeld's drug store sign is simpler, but is still standing even though the mom-and-pop store is out of business.

At one time, travelers could just follow this arrow and find North Lima Pharmacy in Mahoning County, Ohio. Now, however, the barn is no longer where it once stood. It was destroyed by fire in 2003.

The barn inset advertised pianos for several years before being torn down, while the barn above still touts First National Bank in Gallia County, Ohio, for those who can make out its disappearing sign.

First painted in 1976 as part of the nation's bicentennial celebration, this central Ohio barn recently was repainted all white—covering up the red-white-and-blue Pepsi signs.

These are archival images of Dr. Pierce's barns as well as a Pennsylvania barn that still lets passersby know about his medicinal products. *Images at right: Author's collection, Library of Congress*

It only took a three-digit phone number to reach horse dealer George McKee, as this barn in Noble County, Ohio, attests.

Above: This barn pitching Koehler Beer was restored in Erie, Pennsylvania, even though the area brewery is no longer in business. Residents wanted to keep a piece of local history alive. *Right:* A Golden Age beverage sign fills the side of this barn in Columbiana County, Ohio.

A fading Royal Crown Cola sign can still be seen on this Kentucky barn on Route 460 in Morgan County.

CHAPTER FIVE

Fading, But Not Forgotten

The golden age of painting barns ended in 1965 as a result of Congress passing the Highway Beautification Act. When that legislation passed, many of these simple eye-catching messages, which at the time were considered nothing more than billboards, were painted over. Since then, many of the barns have been torn down. Others have simply never been repainted, and their messages—under the glare of the sun and weathered by snow, wind, and rain—have faded with each passing season.

But as many of these visual time capsules disappeared, more and more people became interested in saving the ones that remained. Congress also switched its position on the barns that lawmakers once deemed eyesores. In May 2002, President George W. Bush signed the Historic Barn Preservation Act, legislation that helped states protect barns that are 50-plus years old from being demolished, including ones with advertising signs. With the legislation came a program geared to educate the public on the histories of these barns, the construction techniques used to build them, and the role they played in the agricultural prosperity of this country. Another national program, BARN AGAIN!, is also working to preserve the historic barns and rural buildings that are sponsored by the National Trust for Historic Preservation and *Successful Farming* magazine. BARN AGAIN! offers up-to-date information to the owners of these barns so they can rehabilitate them and make them usable for modern-day farming and ranching operations.

Opposite: Only very faint outlines of lettering are still visible on this barn in southern Ohio. *Above:* Passersby might have to look closely at this barn, too, but the prices of suits and overcoats are still visible from Route 68 in Champaign County, Ohio.

This tattered barn in Centre County, Pennsylvania, once was home to a much bolder advertisement for The Big Store, which sold clothing and other assorted goods.

The Cottage Grove Historical Society in Oregon decided that this Dr. Pierce's Pleasant Pellets barn could not fade away, so the group's members had the sign repainted to preserve it.
Gene Spears

Historical societies and other grass-roots movements have also gotten behind the idea of restoring these rural landmarks. In 1993, longtime Mail Pouch painter Harley Warrick came out of retirement to repaint a wonderful red barn on the outskirts of Lanesville, Indiana. He was persuaded by the Lanesville Heritage Committee, which had purchased the barn and wanted to make sure Warrick had one more chance to share his art. In Cottage Grove, Oregon, the local historical society decided that an advertising barn in that community could not be lost to the ravages of time.

Society members rallied to restore the "Dr. Pierce's Pleasant Pills for Your Liver" message for future generations to enjoy. When it came to saving the two remaining Meramec Cavern barns on historic Route 66 in Illinois, the Mother Road's preservation group stepped in. Volunteers for the organization even repainted the barns themselves, climbing the scaffold just like the paint signers did during the Depression era.

The effort hasn't been limited to preserving old advertising barns, though. Some businesses have decided to rekindle this quaint form of advertising and have commissioned a barn or two to be painted in the style that was so popular from the 1920s to the mid-1960s. Bob Evans restaurants, with headquarters in Ohio, chose two barns to host its advertisements, a move the restaurant chain's executives saw as fitting in well with the restaurant's down-home image. One of these barns, with a large colorful sign on its roof, can be seen on I-65 near Columbus, Indiana. But the contract for the sign ended in 1999 because Bob Evans executives felt the barn was too far off the road, and the structure was no longer safe to scale and paint. The other barn with a Bob Evans advertisement, located north of Decatur, Illinois, was discontinued in 2001. Both signs will someday fade away or be torn down. Another Ohio company that has recently used barns to advertise is the Kiko Auction Company, located in Canton, Ohio. Kiko hired Ohio bicentennial barn painter Scott Hagen to complete the job for its advertising barns. The first two barns were painted around the year 2000 and proved to be successful in attracting the rural customers that the auction/real estate company wanted to serve. A third roadside barn sign was finished in 2003. Like the arrangements of the past, a trade was made with the farmer, a freshly painted barn for the use of a well-placed advertisement. Time will tell if more Kiko Auction barns will appear on curvy country roads.

An original Rock City barn along Highway 41 in Sevierville, Tennessee, also got a fresh new coat of paint as

Kiko Auction Company of Canton, Ohio, has made barn advertising part of its modern marketing efforts by having three signs painted across the region. This one is on Route 172 in Columbiana County.

Bob Evans Restaurants tried the barn advertising route in the 1990s, but decided to end the promotion. This one is along Interstate 65 in Bartholomew, Indiana.

Hillside Tobacco barns are a scarce sight, and soon will be scarcer when the lettering on this one in Indiana wears away.

part of Hampton Inn's "Explore the Highway with Hampton, Save a Landmark" program. The barn was erected in the early 1940s and became Hampton's second landmark refurbishment. Volunteers and Hampton employees rebuilt walls and doors, worked on the roof, and repainted the old Rock City sign that appears on the front of the barn.

All of these barns were created or restored because those who love history have decided that these rural relics shouldn't fade into oblivion. They know that if more of them vanish, the story of these old barns will never be told. And sadly, many of the barns' original artisans—such as Maurice Zimmerman, Harley Warrick, and Clark Byers—are no longer here to tell about the days they spent painting these simple signs. The only things left of this era are the hundreds of barns that can still be found on our country's roads. Charming, nostalgic, and classic—they won't last forever. Except maybe in our memories.

This Meramec Caverns barn and the one in the photo below are the only two remaining ones on Route 66 in Illinois. Because they are a part of the history of the Mother Road, the Route 66 Association of Illinois restored both of them. *Peter Stork*

This Meramec Caverns sign on Route 62 in Perry County, Indiana, would be easy to miss, though, as it's now covered by greenery.

Right: Vanishing Country Ham and Mail Pouch signs cover this barn on Route 31E in Hart County, Kentucky. *Below:* This Pennsylvania barn is no longer standing. At one time, it had both Mail Pouch and a brand of ginger ale signs.

Both these barns are home to signs that are quickly disappearing. The red barn at left has pitched Richman's Clothes for decades and the one below really can't be deciphered.

Ohio Bicentennial Barns

Ohioans wanted to find a special way to celebrate their state's 200th birthday in 2003. And because their state is home to many advertising barns, members of the state's bicentennial commission decided in 1998 that painting barns would be an appropriate way to commemorate Ohio's official entrance into the United States. So the goal became to paint a red-white-and-blue Ohio bicentennial logo on one barn in each of the state's 88 counties.

The commission used tried-and-true methods when selecting the barns that eventually would display these logos. Members wanted barns that were in good condition, faced a well-traveled road, and already had a base coat of paint. Nearly 2,000 barn owners offered their barns for the job.

The commission chose Scott Hagen, the only artist to paint all of these Ohio barns, because of his prior barn-painting work—adding sports team logos to the large rural structures. Hagen was destined for the job because he hailed from Belmont County, the home of the most famous barn painter, Harley Warrick. Before Warrick passed away in November 2000, he offered Hagen some painting pointers and loaned him the use of his scaffold.

As Hagen traveled from county to county to complete the project, his barn painting visits became highly antici-pated events. Volunteers often helped prep the soon-to-be painted barns before he arrived.

Opposite: For its bicentennial, members of Ohio's bicentennial commission decided that they wanted barns in each county to be painted as part of the festivities. This is the barn that was painted in Washington County. *Above:* This one on Munson Road was selected as Lake County's landmark.

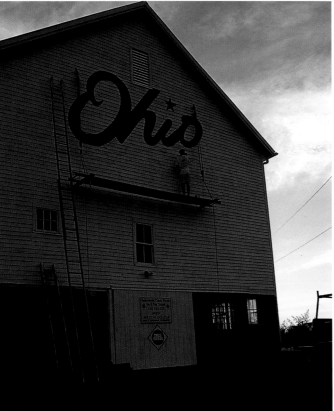

When he was all set to begin, there were usually many families sitting nearby, picnic lunches on hand, ready to watch him work. Schools and Scout troops also scheduled field trips to see him in action. Throughout Hagen's 18-hour process of freehand painting the 20-square foot logo, newspaper and television reporters documented his progress, taking photographs and soliciting impressions from the crowd. Eventually, admirers started county-by-county tours to get a glimpse of Hagen's work.

Unfortunately, one barn Hagen completed wasn't around long enough for many people to see. The 100-year-old Ottawa County barn was a victim of Mother Nature. A tornado destroyed it only about 30 minutes after Hagen finished painting it.

The rest, though, were still standing when the state's bicentennial celebration began. They served as a reminder that farming played a large role in Ohio's economic history and that these barns, as well as the older historic advertising barns, are a big part of that history. Here is a sampling Hagen's work.

Above and at left: Scott Hagen paints the Ohio bicentennial logo on a barn in Geauga County. It was the 22nd barn to receive the symbol.

The barn in Belmont County, Ohio, home to both legendary barn painter Harley Warrick and Scott Hagen, was chosen as the first barn to be painted as part of the bicentennial barn program.

The red barn above can be seen from Interstate 71 in Delaware County, while the one at right is off Route 33 in Hocking County, Ohio.

Glints of sunlight strike the side of this Ohio bicentennial barn near Insterstate 77 in Tuscarawas County.

A rainbow pops out of the gray clouds and surrounds this Ashland County bicentennial barn.

Acknowledgments

Thank you to the many individuals and organizations who assisted me in putting this book together. I especially appreciate the many advertising barn owners who allowed me to photograph their barns.

The following people have my heartfelt gratitude for their help and support: Leah Noel and Lee Klancher at Motorbooks International; Norman and Gladys Zimmerman for sharing their family's photo album and his father Maurice's story; the late Harley Warrick, for time spent in his workshop chatting with him and listening to his stories. Thanks also go to Rock City Gardens; Les Turilla of Meramec Caverns; Mary Ruth Whorton at the Mail Pouch Tobacco Company; the people from the West Virginia Division of Culture and History; the Ohio County Public Library; Wheeling, West Virginia; the Mary H. Weir Public Library, Weirton, West Virginia; the Ohio Historical Society; the Maryland State Archives; Bowling Green State University Center for Archival Collections; and The Library of Congress. Many thanks also go to Carla Simmonds, for countless hours spent driving as I searched for barns; Gail Norris; Richard Simmonds; Pat and Nancy Kilkenny; Allen Boley; Steve McKee; Glen Fero; Werner Lindquist; Ray Day; Peter Stork; Gene Spears; Tom Plimpton; Mike MacCarter and Ohiobarns.com; and the many people who supplied me with barn locations and encouragement.

Index